MW01490353

My SOJOURN in HEAVEN and STOPOVER in HELL

By John Bunyan

**Edited by
Mary Stewart Relfe, Ph.D.**

My Sojourn in Heaven and Stopover in Hell

By
John Bunyan

Edited By
Mary Stewart Relfe

ISBN: 0-9607986-3-3
Printed in the United States of America
Copyright © 1997 by League of Prayer, Inc.

League of Prayer
P.O. Box 680310
Prattville AL 36068
Phone 334-361-8497

Text, earlier published by Osterhus Publishing House, 4500 West Broadway, Minneapolis, MN 55422, has been edited only to reduce length of sentences, divide into paragraphs, and affix topics and subtopics in order that this generation "*can read it at a glance and rush to tell others,*" Hab. 2:2 TLB. Selected inserts, separated from text, have been added for enrichment.

APPRECIATION

To
Martha Medders Headley, **B.A., M.Ed.,**
former Alabama public school teacher, missionary
to Belize, life-long friend, and colleague for years at
League of Prayer, for typesetting, proofing, and cri-
tiquing this manuscript. Without her assistance and
promptings, the project would not have been brought
to fruition.

Cover Design

Deborah Evans
Oceanside, CA 92056

About the Editor

Dr. Mary Stewart Relfe has authored several books. Two were #1 bestsellers, *When Your Money Fails*, (1981), and *The New Money System*, (1982). Both were translated into several foreign languages. She also wrote a bestseller, *Cure of All Ills — Revival*, (1988).   Since 1981 she has served as editor/writer of a newsletter which goes into all the English speaking world — at one time translated into Norwegian and Afrikaans.

Dr. Relfe is a minister with credentials in the Assemblies of God. She has been a pulpit guest in the largest church in the world, Yoido Full Gospel, Seoul, Korea at the invitation of Dr. David Yonggi Cho two successive years.   She has been guest speaker at statewide prayer/revival seminars, ministered at Headquarters Chapel of the Assemblies of God in Springfield, MO, (1995), and Church of God Headquarters Church, Cleveland, TN, (1986).

She has spoken in many different churches in the Western world, Asia and Europe.

She is the widow of the late Dr. C.B. Relfe, a Montgomery physician.

About the Publisher

League of Prayer, Inc. was founded in 1980 by Dr. Mary Stewart Relfe. She serves as President/CEO of *League of Prayer, USA*, an IRS-approved, tax-exempt 501(c)3 religious/humanitarian agency, headquartered in Montgomery, AL, and *League of Prayer-Russia*, registered and headquartered in Moscow Central Hospital, Moscow, Russia. The ministry publishes books and newsletters, sponsors missionaries and provides Bibles, books, food, clothes and medicines locally and in many nations.

League of Prayer-Russia operates that nation's largest soup kitchen and only Christian preschool, goes into 400 prisons, children's hospitals and has distributed in excess of 250,000 Bibles and New Testaments there since 1992.

League of Prayer
P.O. Box 680310
Prattville AL 36068
Phone 334-361-8497

Ph⟨   ⟨4

Prayer

Now may this little book a blessing be,
To those that love this little book and me,
And may its buyer have no cause to say,
His money is but lost or thrown away.

And may it persuade some that go astray,
To turn their foot and heart to the right way.

Is the Hearty Prayer
of the Author
John Bunyan

CONTENTS

DEDICATION

To Younger Generation —

Deceived by Satan-pleasing, "enlightened" educators, who have fashioned an amoral, empty,
joyless society
where prevails
no reverence for God
no dread of the Devil,
no assurance of Heaven,
and
no fear of dying.

May this divinely granted expose of insights into
the spiritual realm compensate for the perversion of
reality;
May *the eyes of your understanding be enlightened* as you read of this incredible trip — God
endorsed, not drug-induced;
and
May these revelations ignite your quest for truth
until you declare like King David —

O how I love Thy law . . .

*Thy commandments have made me wiser
than my enemies . . .*

*I have more understanding than all my
teachers . . .*

*I understand more than the ancients,
because I keep Thy precepts.*

Psalm 119:97-100

Introduction

John Bunyan, from traveling tinker to mighty minister, whom God used to change the destiny of his generation.

John was tall, big-boned, and of ruddy complexion . . .He had a large mouth, a high forehead and piercing eyes. He wore a British mustache and plain attire.

Early years

Bunyan was born in Elstow, a stone's throw from Bedford, England. His father was a "tinker," traveling from door to door repairing pots and pans. The family had owned land in Bedfordshire since the 12th century.

Despite their lowliness, his parents paid special attention to John's training, and unlike most boys of his day, they sent him to a grammar school in Bedford for a short while. He also learned and practiced his father's trade.

Two marriages

Bunyan served as a soldier in 1645-1646 during the Civil War. At age 20, he married an orphan girl, *"not having so much as a dish or spoon."* He never mentions her name. The wife's dowry consisted of two books, *The Plain Man's Pathway to Heaven* and *The Practice of Piety.* These books in no small measure awakened Bunyan spiritually.

The couple had four children, two girls and two boys. The oldest child, Mary, was born blind. His first wife died in 1658. The following year he married again, and "Elizabeth" was a most devoted wife and mother. They had two children.

"Soul darkness"

John experienced an intense spiritual conflict as a youth. He was fond of dancing, bell ringing and sports on the village green. While having strong religious feelings, he admits: *"Even as a child, I had few equals in cursing, swearing, lying and blaspheming the holy name of God."* In his autobiography he looked back on himself in youth as *"the very ringleader of all . . . that kept me company into all manner of vice and ungodliness."*

After his first marriage, he began attending church. One Sunday, after the sermon, he went out to play a game of "tipcat." About to strike the cat, a voice spoke, *"Wilt thou leave thy sins and go to Heaven, or have thy sins and go to Hell?"* He looked up to Heaven and saw Christ looking down sternly upon him.

John believed that he had committed the unpardonable sin, and in desperation returned to his pleasures of games and dancing.

Some *"friends"* began insisting there was no Heaven, Hell, God, or the Devil. Beginning to doubt that there was a Hell, he suddenly *"found the flames of it flashing in his face."*

Having reached the *"utmost pitch of desperation,"* he decided to *"put a period to this wretched life."* He took a lethal weapon to nearby woods where he fully intended to kill himself. But a voice spoke, " *. . . That fatal stroke thou art about to give seals thy damnation. For if there be a God, how can you hope for mercy from Him when you willfully destroy His image?"*

Angel appears

He fell on his knees and praised this merciful Lord who had prevented his suicide. Taking a seat on a nearby bank, a glorious light surrounded him. It took the form of a man. This Angel, *Shining Deliverer*, explained to him that he was sent to show Bunyan the realities of those things he had questioned. The method God chose was for the Angel to conduct him on a tour to Heaven, Hell and back to the earth.

This book is about that *journey of journeys*, though Bunyan admits that he can only speak *"imperfectly of it . . . and cannot tell the thousandth part."*

Ministry emerges

After John's aborted suicide attempt, conversion, visitation in Heaven and Hell, Bunyan added two more books to his library, *Foxe's Book of Martyrs* and the *King James Bible*.

He read the Bible until his tongue became *"Elizabethan."* He preached with such fervor and eloquence that many flocked to hear him. Fresh from his own "storms of temptation," he felt fitted to warn and console others.

"I went myself in chains to preach to them in chains, and carried that fire in my own conscience that I persuaded them to be aware of."

"All the midland counties heard of his fame and demanded to hear him," said James Froude.

The Restoration of Charles II brought to an end the 20 years in which the *separated* churches had enjoyed freedom.

Imprisonment

On November 12, 1660, Bunyan was brought before a local magistrate and, under an old Elizabethan act, charged with holding a service not in conformity with the Church of England. Refusing to agree not to preach again, he was condemned at the assizes and imprisoned in the County Jail in Bedford for three months. In spite of courageous efforts of his second wife to have the case brought up for trial, he remained in prison unjustly for 12 years, (1660-1672).

While in prison, he provided for his family by making "*many hundred gross of long tagged laces for boots.*"

John was offered his freedom several times upon the condition he would preach no more. His reply was always the same, "*You release me today; I'll preach tomorrow.*"

His confinement was of advantage to him. Here he "*dreamed dreams and saw visions.*" His bonds too fell "*out rather unto the furtherance of the Gospel.*"

Literary activity

It was in Bedford *Gaol* that Bunyan mastered the Scriptures. Here also he penned his autobiography, *Grace Abounding to the Chief of Sinners*, (1666). Probably much of Pilgrim's Progress was written here, (1678).

The world can be thankful he received little education. This enabled him to become an original and creative thinker, finally producing the world's first novel, *Pilgrim's Progress*. This book was instantly popular with all classes, though it was perhaps the last great expression of folk tradition before the divisive effects of modern "enlightened" education.

Pilgrim's Progress has crossed racial and cultural lines, and acquired the epithet, *"the lay Bible."* It is remarkable for its simplicity, imaginative fervor, and universality of its spiritual appeal. No book has been more widely accepted and freer from sectarian dogmas.

Rousing preacher

Upon release from his unjust imprisonment, Bunyan received a license to preach, along with 25 other noncomformists. He became the organizing genius of the dissenters and earned the title *"Bishop Bunyan."*

In 1672 he was elected pastor of the Bedford Church. From this time (except for a six month re-imprisonment in 1677 which he served in the jail over Bedford Bridge), he was busy preaching and writing. His influence from these activities made him *"second to scarcely any man in England."*

Death

He died prematurely August 31, 1688, in his 60th year. Having gone to Reading, he successfully reconciled a father and son. While continuing his journey to London, he was overtaken by a rainstorm. His death resulted from the effects of the exposure.

Reputation

John was rightly named. He was another *"Son of Thunder,"* who, in his short life, caused a spiritual and moral earthquake that rearranged human landscape.

———————

"Until the decline of religious faith, Bunyan, like the Bible, was to be found in every English home . . . In literary estimation . . . he was acknowledged by Swift and Johnson, recognized as a natural genius, and placed alongside Homer and Robert Burns."
—Encyclopaedia Britannica

MARY STEWART RELFE

" . . . *Ye shall live also.* "
John 14:19

O world of wonders! (I can say no less)
That I should be preserved in that distress
That I have met with here! O blessed be
That hand that from it hath delivered me!

Dangers in darkness, devils, Hell, and sin,
Did compass me, while I this Vale was in;

Yea, snares, and pits, and traps,
    and nets did lie
My path about, that worthless silly I
Might have been catched, entangled,
    and cast down:
But since I live, let JESUS wear the Crown!

John Bunyan

"Come unto me . . . "
Mat. 11:28

Would'st thou read and know'st not what
Or yet whether thou art blest or not,
Come read these lines, O come hither,
And lay my book, thy head and heart together.

John Bunyan

Chapter I

Suicide Averted by Divine Intervention

When wicked persons have gone on in a life of sin, and find they have reason to fear the just judgment of God for their sins, they begin at first to wish that there were no God to punish them. Then, by degrees, they persuade themselves that there is none. They set themselves to study for arguments to back their opinion. It is with one of this sort of men that I had the unhappiness to be acquainted. He was continually impressing me that there was neither God nor Devil, Heaven, nor Hell.

It was not without horror and trembling that I first heard this. Therefore I usually left him when he began upon these topics. But his speaking of them to me so often at last prevailed with me to consider what grounds he had for what he said. From this time I found my mind perplexed with so much trouble and darkness that I could hardly bear up under it. I knew not how to make out to my own satisfaction these truths which before appeared to me self-evident. I could not think there was no God except with the greatest horror. Yet, I called in question the truth of His being. I would not have parted with my hope of Heaven had I been made heir of all the world. Yet, I questioned whether there was any such place or state. I began to doubt whether there was any Hell, and at the same time, thought I found "*the flames of it flashing in my face.*" Thus was my mind tossed with apparent contradictions, and I found myself confused.

The choice of friends should be made with great care. They can be the fairest furniture of life or the worst stool in the parlor.

Bad influence of "good" friend

In this perplexed condition, I went to my false friend to see what comfort he would give to me. He indeed laughed at my fears, pretended to pity my weakness, and seemed to hug himself in the freedom and liberty which he enjoyed. He told me he was never bothered by the frightful anticipations of a future state, or an after-reckoning. Nature was the great mistress of the universe and therefore he followed her dictates. All the care he took was to live here. He hoped that when his dust should be next impregnated, it would be into some delightful species of beings which would, in a great measure, be owing to the place of his burial.

These talks of his put me to doubting even more. I became so uneasy that my life was a burden to me. I dreaded to be left to the belief of those cursed notions, yet they continually ran in my mind. I wished a thousand times I had never heard them, yet they were ever before me. Are all my hopes of Heaven nothing but a vain dream? Have I served God for nothing? Or rather have I fancied One when there is no such being? It is impossible to tell the agonies I felt upon my giving way to such thoughts as these. Still with greater force they assaulted me, until at last I was hurried to the utmost *pitch of desperation*. Why should I linger thus, I thought, between despair and hope? Is it not better, I said to myself, to put a *period to this wretched life* and to try the truth of things?

"A still small voice"

Upon this I took a resolution to destroy myself. In order to do this, I went out one morning to nearby woods, where I intended to act out this bloody tragedy. But methought I heard a *secret whisper* saying:

> *"O Epenetus, (Bunyan), plunge not thyself in everlasting misery to gratify thy soul's worst enemy. That fatal stroke thou art about to give seals up thine own damnation. For if there be a God, as surely there is, how can you hope for mercy from Him when you thus willfully destroy His image?"*

Whence this secret whisper came I knew not, but I believe it was from God. It came with so much power it made me fling away the instrument with which I had intended to do violence to my own life and showed me in a moment the wickedness thereof. The horror of this awful intention set all my joints a-trembling, so that I could hardly stand. I could not but acknowledge my deliverance to be the work of some *Invisible and Spiritual Power* that came to my rescue. Now gratitude obliged me to return thanks to Him.

Doxology in prayer

I kneeled down on the ground and said: *"O Thou Invisible, Eternal Power, which though unseen by men beholdest all his actions and who hast now withheld me from defacing Thine image, I give Thee humble thanks. Yes, O Thou Sovereign Being of All Beings, I give Thee thanks that I am still alive and able to acknowledge there is such a Being. Oh, let the Sun of Glory shine upon me and chase away the blackness of my soul. Let me never more question Thy Being or Omnipotence, which I have this moment so greatly experienced."*

Angelic visitation

Then, rising from my knees, I went and sat down on a bank. My mind was greatly taken up with the adoring thoughts of the Eternal Goodness. He had saved me from the dreadful gulf of everlasting ruin, just when I was going to plunge myself into it. Now I could only wonder that I should be such a fool as to call in question the being of the Deity which every creature was witness of, and which a man's own conscience could not but dictate to him.

Now while my thoughts were taken up as I sat upon the bank, I was suddenly surrounded with a glorious light. The exceeding brightness of this was such as I had never seen before. It both surprised and amazed me. While I was wondering whence it came, I saw coming toward me a *Glorious Appearance*, like the person of a man, but circled round about with beams of inexpressible light and glory. These streamed from him all the way as he came. His countenance was very awful, and yet mixed with such an air of sweetness as rendered it extremely pleasing, and gave me some secret hope that he came not to me as an enemy. Yet I knew not how to bear his bright appearance. Endeavoring to stand upon my feet, I soon found I had no more strength in me, and so fell down flat on my face. By the kind assistance of his arm, I was soon set upon my feet again, and new strength was put into me. Then I addressed myself to the Bright Form before me, saying, *"O my Shining Deliverer, who hast strengthened my feeble body and restored me to new life, how shall I acknowledge my thankfulness, and in what manner shall I adore thee?"*

To which he replied, both with an air of majesty and mildness, *"Pay thy adorations to the Author of thy being, and not to me who am thy fellow-creature. I am sent by Him Whose very Being thou hast so lately denied, to stop thee from falling into that eternal ruin whereinto thou wert going to throw thyself."*

This touched my heart with such a sense of my own unworthiness that my soul even melted within. I could not forbear crying out, *"Oh, how utterly unworthy I am of all this grace and mercy!"*

To this the Heavenly Messenger replied: *"The divine Majesty shows mercy, not according to thy unworthiness, but His Own unbounded goodness and vast love. He saw with how much malice the grand enemy of souls desires thy ruin. He let him go on with hopes of overcoming thee, yet upheld thee by His secret power. When Satan thought himself most sure, the snare is broken, and thou art escaped.*" These words made me break forth in rapture:

Oh, who the depths of this great love can tell,
To save a tempted sinking soul from Hell!
Oh, glory, glory to my Savior's name
I'll now through all eternity proclaim!
Who, when I on the brink of ruin lay,
Saved me from him who would my soul betray.
And now I know, though I no God would own,
The Lord is God; yea, He is God alone!

"I lifted up mine eyes and looked, and behold a certain man . . . as the appearance of lightning . . . and there remained no strength in me . . . When I heard the voice of his words, then was I in a deep sleep on my face, and my face toward the ground.

"And behold a hand touched me . . . and he said unto me . . . stand upright . . . And when he had spoken this word unto me, I stood trembling."

Dan. 10:5-11 excerpts

"Ministers of Christ . . .
Stewards of the mysteries of God."
I Cor. 4:1

"I have yet many things to say unto you, but
you cannot bear them now."
John 16:12

This book will make a traveller of thee,
If by its counsel thou wilt ruled be;
It will direct thee to the Holy Land,
If thou wilt its directions understand:
Yea, it will make the slothful active be,
The blind also **delightful things to see**.

John Bunyan

Who search for Truth and do not start from God
For a long, long journey must be shod.

Coventry Patmore

Chapter II

Things Never Beheld by Mortal Eye

This Heavenly Visitor said with a pleasing countenance, "that you may never doubt anymore the reality of eternal things, the end of my coming to you is to convince you of the truth of them. This will not be accomplished by **faith only** but by **sight also! For I will show you such things as were never yet beheld by mortal eye!** To that end your eyes shall be strengthened and made fit to behold immaterial objects."

At these surprising words of the Angel I was much astonished, and doubted how I should be able to bear it. I said to him, "O my Lord, who is sufficient to bear such a sight?" To which he replied, "The joy of the Lord shall be your strength."

When he had said thus, he took hold of me and said, "Fear not; for I am sent to show the **things thou hast not seen**."

Up, up and away

Before I was aware, I found myself far above the earth, which seemed to me a very small point in comparison with that region of light into which I was translated. Then I said to my *Bright Conductor*, "Oh, let it not offend my lord if I ask a question or two of thee."

To this he answered, "Speak on. It is my work to inform thee of such things which thou shalt inquire of me. For *I am a Ministering Spirit, sent forth to minister to thee and to those that shall be heirs of salvation*."

Earth — "little dark spot"

I then said, "I would fain be informed what that *dark spot*, so far below me, is. It has grown less and less as I have mounted higher and higher, and appears much darker since I have come into this region of light."

"That little spot," answered my Conductor, "that now looks so dark and contemptible, is that world of which you were so recently an inhabitant. Here you may see how little all that world appears. For a small part so many men have run the hazard of losing, nay, have actually lost, their precious and immortal souls — souls so precious that the Prince of Peace has told us that though one man could gain the whole, it could not recompense so great a loss.

"And also, the great reason of their folly is that they did not look to things above. For as you ascended nearer to this region, the world appeared still less and the more contemptible. And it will do the same to all who can, by faith, once get their hearts above it.

"Could the inhabitants below but see the world just as it is, they would not covet it as they now do. But they are in a state of darkness. And this is worse, they love to walk therein! For though the Prince of Light came down among them and plainly showed them the true Light of Life, yet they go on in darkness and will not bring themselves into the light, because their deeds are evil."

"Wicked spirits in high places," Eph. 6:12

I inquired of my Bright Conductor, "What are those multitudes of black and horrid forms that hover in the air above the world. Indeed I would have been much afraid of, but they fled as you passed by — perhaps not being able to abide in the brightness with which you are arrayed?"

To this he answered me, "They were the fallen and Apostate Spirits which for their pride and rebellion were cast down from Heaven. They wander in the air by the decree of the Almighty. These are bound in chains of darkness and kept unto the judgment of the great day."

Two-fold purpose

The Angel continued, "From thence, however, they are permitted to descend into the world, both for the *trial of the Elect and for the condemnation of the wicked*. Though you now see they have black and horrid forms, yet they were once the Sons of Light, arrayed in robes of glorious brightness like what you see me wear. Indeed, it was the loss of this, though it was the effect of their own willful sin, which fills them with rage and malice against the ever Blessed God Whose power and majesty they fear and hate."

Why they were condemned and man was redeemed

"Tell me," I said, "O Happy Conductor, have they no hopes of being reconciled to God again, after some term of time, or at least some of them?"

"No, not at all. They are lost forever. They were the first that sinned, and *they had no tempter*! They were all at once cast down from Heaven.

"Besides, the Son of God, the Blessed Messiah, by Whom alone salvation can be had, took not upon Him the angelic nature, but left the Apostate Angels all to perish. He took upon Himself only the seed of Abraham. For this reason they have so much malice against the sons of men, whom it is a torment to them to see made heirs of Heaven, while they are doomed to Hell."

Close-up of the sun and stars

Our position now was above the sun. Its vast and glorious body was so much greater than the earth. It moved round the great expanse wherein it was placed with such a mighty swiftness that to relate it would appear incredible. But my Conductor told me this mighty immense hanging globe of fire was just one of the great works of God! It always keeps its constant course. It never has the least irregularity in its daily or its annual motion. It is so exceedingly glorious in its body that had not my eyes been greatly strengthened, I could not have beheld it.

There were those mighty globes of fire we call the fixed stars no less wonderful. Their vast and extreme height, so many leagues above the sun, makes them appear like candles in our sight. Yet they hang within their spheres without any support, *in a pure sea of ether*. Nothing but His Word that first created them could keep them in their station.

"These words are enough," I said to my Conductor, "to convince anyone of the great power of their much more adorable Creator, and also of the blackness of that infidelity which can call in question the being of a Deity who has given the whole world so many bright evidences of His power and glory. If men were not like beasts still looking downwards, they could not help but acknowledge His great power and wisdom."

Arrival in Glory

"You speak what is true," replied my Conductor. "But you shall see far greater things than these. These are all but the **scaffolds** and **outworks** to that glorious building wherein the Blessed above inhabit — 'that house not made with hands, eternal in the Heavens.' This *view* (as far as you are capable to comprehend it) shall now be given you."

Within moments, what I had been told by my Conductor I found good. I was presently transferred into the glorious mansions of the Blessed. I saw such things as it is impossible to represent. I heard that ravishing melodious harmony that I can never utter. Well, therefore, might the Beloved Apostle John tell us in his Epistle: "Now are we the sons of God; and it doth not yet appear what we shall be."

"Not possible to utter," II Cor. 12:4

Whoever has not seen that glory can speak out very *imperfectly of it*. They that have, *cannot tell the thousandth part* of what it is. Therefore the great Apostle of the Gentiles, who tells us he had been caught up into Paradise, where he had heard unspeakable words which is not possible for a man to utter, gives us no other account of it, but that —

> "Eye hath not seen, nor ear heard, nor has it entered into the heart of man to conceive the things that God has laid up for those that love Him," I Cor. 2:9.

Those things being as they are, I will give you the best account I can of what I saw and heard, of the blessed discourses I had with some of the Blessed, as near as I can remember.

"In My Father's House are many mansions . . . I go to prepare a place for you."
> John 14:2

"And without controversy, great is the mystery of godliness,"
> I Tim. 3:16.

33

The immortal realm

*And it came to pass . . . He took Peter, John
and James and went up into a mountain to pray.*

*And as He prayed, the fashion of His counte-
nance was altered, and His raiment was white and
glistering.*

*And, behold, there talked with him two men,
which were Moses and Elijah, who appeared in
glory, and spoke of His decease . . .*

Luke 9:28-31   excerpts

May I now enter here? Will he within
Open to sorry me, though I have been
An undeserving rebel? Then shall I,
Not fail to sing his praise on high.

John Bunyan

SURELY God would not have created
such a being as man, with an ability to grasp
the infinite, to exist only for a day! No, no,
man was made for immortality.

Abraham Lincoln

Chapter III

Elijah Talks Again

When I was first brought near this *glorious palace*, I saw innumerable hosts of Bright Attendants. They welcomed me into the blissful seat of happiness. All their countenances had an air of perfect joy and of the highest satisfaction.

There I saw that perfect and unapproachable light that assimilates all things into its own nature. Even the souls of the Glorified Saints are transparent. Neither are they enlightened by the sun. All that light which flows with so much transparent brightness throughout those heavenly mansions is nothing else but emanations of the Divine Glory. By comparison to this Glory, the light of the sun is but darkness!

Alas, all the luster of the most sparkling diamonds, the fire of carbuncles, sapphires, and rubies, and the orient brightness of the richest pearl are but dead coals in comparison. Therefore it is called

35

the Throne of the Glory of God, wherein the radiant luster of the Divine Majesty is revealed in the most illustrious manner.

God's Glory "unviewable"

Deity, exalted on the high Throne of His glory, receives the adoration of myriads of Angels and Saints. They sing forth eternal hallelujahs and praises to Him, who is too bright an object for mortality to view. Well may He therefore be called the God of Glory, for by His glorious presence He makes Heaven what it is — *rivers of pleasures perpetually springing from the divine Presence and radiating cheerfulness, joy, and splendor to all the Blessed Inhabitants of Heaven,* the place of His happy residence and seat of His eternal empire.

No dying there

For my own part, my eye was so far too weak to bear the least beautiful ray shot from that everlasting Spring of Light and Glory which sat upon the Throne. I was forced to cry to my Conductor, "The sight of so much glory is too great for frail mortality to bear, yet is so refreshing and delightful that I fain would behold it, though I die."

"No, no," said my Conductor, "death enters not within this blessed place. Here life and immortality reside; nor sin nor sorrow here have ought to do. For it is the glory of this happy place to be forever freed from all that is evil. Without that freedom, our blessedness even here would be imperfect."

Elijah still in body

My Conductor spoke further, "Come along with me and I will bring thee to one that is **in the body, as thou art**. With him converse a while, and then I will reconduct thee back again."

Mansions ready

"O rather," said I with some eagerness, "let me stay here; for here is no need of building tabernacles. The heavenly **mansions are here ready fitted**." My Shining Messenger replied, "Here in a while thou shalt be fixed forever; but *the divine will first must be obeyed*."

Travel instantaneous

Swift as a thought he presently conveyed me through thousands of those bright and winged spirits. Then he presented me to that Illustrious Saint, the great Elijah. He had lived in the world below so many hundred ages past and gone; and yet me-thought I knew him at first sight.

Celestial introduction

My Conductor said to Elijah, "Here's one, who by the commission from the Imperial Throne has been permitted to survey these realms of light. I have brought him hither to learn from thee wherein its glory and its happiness consist."

"That," said the Prophet, "I shall gladly do. It is our meat and drink in these blessed regions to do the will of God and the Lamb. Here we sing His praises and serve Him with the humblest adoration, saying,

'Blessing, and honor, and glory, and pow-er, be unto Him that sits upon the Throne; and to the Lamb for ever and ever: for He has redeemed us to God by His blood, out of every kindred and tongue, and people and nation, and made us unto our God, kings and priests. Even so, Amen.'"

I likewise added my "Amen" to that of the Holy Prophet.

Elijah then inquired of me on what account this great permission and privilege was given to me. (By which I understand the Saints in Heaven are ignorant of what is done on earth; how then can prayers be directed to them?) I then rehearsed what I have already set in writing, at which the Holy Prophet broke forth into this exclamation:

"Glory forever be given to Him that sits on the throne, and to the Lamb, for His unbounded goodness, and great condescension to the weakness of a poor doubting sinner."

Heaven beyond conception

After these things the Prophet said, "Now give attention to what I shall speak. What you have seen and heard already I am sure you never can relate so as to make it understood, for it is beyond what eye hath seen or ear hath heard, or what the heart of man is able to conceive — I mean of those not yet translated to this glorious state, nor freed from their earthly bodies."

Elijah explained, "My being in the body here is no objection to what I now say. Though it has not been subject to the common lot of mortals, death, yet has it suffered such *a change as has been in some sense equal thereto.* For it is made both spiritual and insensitive, and is now no more capable of any further suffering than those Blessed Angels are that compass round the throne. Yet in this full state of happiness, I cannot utter all that I enjoy, nor do I know what shall yet be enjoyed, for here our happiness is always new."

I then requested of the Blessed Prophet to explain himself. I understood not how happiness could be complete and yet admit of new additions. In the world below we generally think that what is full is completely finished. "I humbly hope," said I, "what I shall say may not be taken as the effect of vain curiosity, but that my understanding may be cultivated, which yet retains but dark ideas of these heavenly things."

The Holy Prophet advised, "To satisfy your doubting soul and to confirm your wavering faith is the chief reason of your being brought hither, through the permission of the great Three One. Therefore, I would have you still, as any doubt arises in your breast, to make it known. But as to that which you inquire, that happiness cannot be complete and yet admit of new additions, I must tell you that when the soul and body both are happy, as mine now are, I count it a complete state of happiness.

"Know that through all the innumerable ages of eternity, it is the soul and body joined together in the blessed *resurrection state* that shall be the continued subject of this happiness. But in respect of the blessed object of it, which is the ever-adorable and Blessed God, in Whose blissful vision this happiness consists, it is forever new. For the divine perfections being infinite, nothing less than eternity can be sufficient to display their glory. This makes our happiness eternally admit of new additions, and by a necessary consequence, our knowledge of it shall be eternally progressive, too."

Paul visited here, too

Elijah then explained, "So, it was not without reason that the Great Apostle of the Gentiles (who, in the days of his mortality, was once admitted hither as you are) affirmed, 'Eye hath not seen, nor hath ear heard, nor can it enter into the heart of man to conceive what God hath prepared for them that love him!'"

Beyond sight

"Yet the eye hath seen many admirable things in nature. It hath seen mountains of crystal and rocks of diamonds. It hath seen mines of gold, and coasts of pearl, and spicy islands. Yet, the eye that hath seen so many wonders in the world below could never pry into the glories of this triumphant state."

Beyond sound

"And yes, the ear of man hath heard many delightful and harmonious sounds. All that art, and that nature could supply him with could not equip him to hear the heavenly melody which here both Saints and Angels make before the Throne."

Beyond fancying

The Prophet adds, "The heart of man is of so fine and curious a composure that it can almost conceive anything that either is, or was, or ever shall be in the world below; yea, what shall never be. Man can conceive that every stone on earth shall be turned into the most orient pearls and every blade of grass into the brightest and most shining jewels. He can conceive that every particle of dust shall be turned into silver and the whole earth into a mass of pure refined gold. He can conceive the air to be turned into a crystal and every star advanced into a sun; and every sun a thousand times more large and glorious than what he now beholds it. Yet this is infinitely short of what the High Eternal Majesty hath prepared for all His faithful followers."

I am content with what I have,
Little be it, or much:
And, Lord, contentment still I crave,
Because thou savest such.

Fullness to such a burden is
That go on pilgrimage:
Here little, and hereafter bliss,
Is best from age to age.

John Bunyan

A man there was,
Though some did count him mad,
The more he cast away,
The more he had.

John Bunyan

He that bestows his goods upon the poor,
Shall have as much again, and ten times more.

John Bunyan

The trials that those men do meet withal
That are obedient to the heavenly call,
Are manifold and suited to the flesh,
And come, and come, and come again afresh;
That now, or sometime else, we by them may
Be taken, overcome, and cast away.
O let the pilgrims, let the pilgrims then
Be vigilant, and quit themselves like men.

John Bunyan

Hidden things revealed

"I have shewed thee new things from this time,
even hidden things, and thou didst not know them."
Isa. 48:6

This place has been our second stage,
Here we have heard and seen
Those good things that from age to age,
To others hid have been.

John Bunyan

Blessed be the day that I began
A Christian for to be;
And blessed also be that man
That thereto moved me.

'Tis true, 'twas long ere I began
To seek to live for ever;
But now I run fast as I can,
'Tis better late than never.

Our tears to joy, our fears to faith
Are turned, as we see:
Thus our beginning (as one saith),
Shows what our end will be.

John Bunyan

Chapter IV

Heaven's Happiness Defined

The prophet Elijah continued his discourse concerning the jubilation of the Glory world. He said, "That you may have the best idea of our happiness, I here will briefly represent unto you what it is those Blessed Souls, who through the glorious purchase of our Bright Redeemer are brought hither, are here delivered from. Though ages spent in this delightful theme would scarce suffice to tell it you at large.

"In order that you might better understand it, I shall endeavor to conform my words to your capacity by comparing things that are here above to what you know below. Your eyes have already told you how infinitely heavenly things transcend whatever can be found on earth. In the second place, I shall represent (as far as your capacity will bear it) what is that happiness the Blessed here enjoy."

Free at last

"First then, the souls of all the blessed are freed forever from whatever it is that can make them miserable, the chief of which you surely know is sin. It is only that which brings the creature into misery.

"The Blessed God, at first, made all things happy; all like Himself, who is supremely so. Had not sin defaced the beauty of Heaven's workmanship, Angels nor men would have never known what is meant by misery. It was sin that threw the Apostate Angels down into Hell and spoiled the beauty of the lower world. It was sin that defaced God's image in man's soul and made the highest order of His creation a slave to his own lust. By so doing, this plunged mankind into an ocean of eternal misery from whence there is no redemption. It is an invaluable mercy that in this happy place all the inhabitants are freed, forever freed, from sin, through the blood of our redeeming Jesus."

From prison bars flown

Further the Holy Prophet said, "In the world below, the best and holiest souls groan underneath the burden of corruption. Sin cleaves to all they do and leads them captive ofttimes against their wills. 'Who shall deliver me?' has been the cry of many of God's faithful servants who at the same time have been dear to Jesus.

"Sin is the heavy clog of Saints themselves while they are embodied in corrupted flesh. Therefore when they lay their bodies down, their souls are like *a bird loosed from its cage* and with a heavenly vigor they mount up to this Blessed Region.

"But up here their warfare is at an end, and 'death is swallowed up in victory.' Here their bright souls, that were below deformed and stained by sin, are by the ever-blessed Jesus presented to the Eternal Father 'without spot or wrinkle.'"

Freed from temptation

"Secondly, here each Blessed Soul is freed from sin; so are they free also from all occasions of it — which is a great addition to our happiness. Adam himself in Paradise, though he was in his first creation perfectly innocent and free from sin, yet was *he not freed from temptations to it*. Satan got into Paradise to tempt him, and he fatally yielded to his temptations. He ate of the forbidden fruit, and fell. By his fall all human nature was corrupted. Sin, like a gangrene, has eaten into the human nature and corrupted all mankind.

"Here each Blessed Soul is likewise freed from this. No devil here can tempt them, nor corruption enter. Nothing but what is pure and holy can find admission here. No sly suggestions from that Apostate Spirit can molest us here. That roaring lion, who is still traversing the earth and seeking whom he may devour, is, with respect to us in this Blessed Region, bound fast in everlasting chains.

"Neither shall the world be any more a tempter to those Blessed Souls who have through faith and patience overcome its wiles and arrived safely here. As strong as its temptations and allurements are to Saints themselves, we that are here, possessors of heavenly mansions, look with contempt on all earthly enjoyments. We here are up above the world and all that it can tempt us with; and through the blood of our triumphing Jesus we have the victory over it. There is nothing here that can disturb our peace, but an eternal calm crowns all our happiness, being freed from sin and all temptations to it."

Freed from sin's ills

The Holy Prophet proceeds with yet more reasons for joyfulness. He declared, "Thirdly, we here are freed from the effects of sin, and it's punishment. Those that are confined to the dark regions of eternal misery are ever groaning under it. The punishment is that which they cannot bear, and yet as that which they must ever suffer. It was sin that ushered death into the world below.

"These are the things which we are in this blessed state delivered from. Yet these make up the least part of the happiness of Heaven. Our joys are positive, as well as negative, and what those are I now proceed to show you."

Happiness interpreted

"All inhabitants here enjoy the sight of God, the Blessed Spring and Eternal Source of all our happiness. But what this is, I can no more declare than can finite creatures comprehend infinity. Only we find that it continually fills our souls with joy unspeakable and full of glory. It is a love so flaming that nothing but the Blessed Author of it can satisfy nor eternity itself can end. It is that which makes us live, and love, and sing, and praise forever. It is that which transforms our souls into His blessed likeness."

Saints below
versus
Redeemed above

"The Saints below, while they are traveling towards this blessed country, are in their pilgrimage supported by His everlasting arms. By this they are enabled to go from grace to grace. But we that are safely landed on the haven of eternal happiness are 'changed from glory to glory even by the Spirit of the Lord.'

"To bring things nearer to your understanding — by the beholding of God's face we have a real enjoyment of His love. His blessed smiles make glad our souls, and in His favor we rejoice continually, 'for in his favor is life.' Then by this blessed vision of God we come to know Him, for *it is a sight of Him that opens our understandings*. It 'gives us the light of the knowledge of the glory of God in the face of Jesus Christ.' Here we all enjoy Him face to face.

"Below the Saints enjoy God in a measure, but here we enjoy Him without measure. There they have some sips of His goodness, but here we have large draughts thereof, and swim in the boundless ocean of happiness. Below, the Saints' communion with God is many times broken off, but here we have an uninterrupted enjoyment of God, **without intermission**. Here we enjoy the perfection of all grace.

"Below love is mixed with fear, and fear hath torment. Here love is perfect, and perfect love casts out fear. Here we love the Blessed God more than ourselves, and one another like ourselves. We here are all the children of one Father, and all our brethren are alike dear unto us. Our knowledge in the world below was very imperfect. Here we see God as He is, and so come to know Him as we are known. Our joy also is here in its perfection."

Minds on earth —
narrow

"Here we have our capacities enlarged, according to the greatness of the objects we have to contemplate. While we were in the world below, no light could shine into our minds but through the windows of our senses. Therefore it was that the Blessed God was pleased to condescend to our capacities and to adapt the expressions of His Majesty to the narrowness of our imaginations.

"But here the revelation of the Deity is much more glorious. Our minds are clarified from all those earthly images that flow through the gross channels of the senses. Below, our purest conceptions of God were very imperfect. But here the gold is separated from the dross, and our conceptions are more proper through the purity of God. Below the objects of glory were humbled to the perceptions of sense. Here the sensible faculties are raised and refined and made the subjects of glory.

"Now therefore since the divine light shines with direct beams, and the *think curtains* of flesh are spiritualized and transparent, the soul enjoys the clearest visions of God. We now see what we before believed of the glorious nature of the ever Blessed God, His decrees and counsels, His providence and dispensations.

"Up here we clearly see that from eternity God was sole existing, but not solitary. We understand that the Godhead is neither confused in unity, nor divided in number. There is a priority of order but no superiority among the sacred persons of the ineffable Trinity. They are equally possessed of the same divine excellencies and the same divine empire. They are also equally the object of the same divine adoration. Those ways of God, that below seemed unsearchable, and that we thought unlawful to inquire into, we here perceive to be the product of divine wisdom, with so much clearness that truth itself is not more evident."

Enoch and Elijah
peculiarly unique

In a different tone the Prophet added, "These things are some of those that constitute our happiness. Yet all these things are only what relate unto our souls. But still the happiness of the inhabitants of this blessed region is not complete until their *bodies are raised and reunited to their souls.*

"Through the divine liberality, *myself and the blessed Enoch do enjoy a more peculiar preference, being translated hither in the body.* We represent types of both the ante- and the post-diluvian world of the resurrection of the ever adorable Son of God, and of all the Saints through Him.

"Now none but the great Messiah has been actually raised from the dead, He being the first fruits thereof. As for Enoch and myself, our bodies have not known death, though they have received a change equivalent thereto. It is therefore most difficult to declare what the resurrection state shall be, being discernible in its perfection only from His glorious body. Neither that of Enoch nor mine are comparable in respect to the glory thereof, though both are *spiritual bodies*, of which I will now show you the distinct properties."

Resurrected body —
as Elijah's

1. "The bodies of the blessed here at the resurrection shall be (as mine is now) *spiritual bodies.* By your not only seeing, but touching me (at which word the Holy Prophet was pleased to give me his hand), you may be the better able to know what I mean by *spiritual body.* That is, a body rarefied from all gross alloys of corruption and made a pure and refined body, and yet a *substantial one,* not composed of wind and air as mortals below are apt to grossly imagine."

Questions please

Here I entreated the Holy Prophet to bear with me. I informed him that I always understood spiritual as opposed to material, and consequently that a spiritual body must be immaterial, and so not capable of being felt as I found his was.

Elijah replied that their bodies were spiritual, not only as they were purified from all corruption, but as they were sustained by the enjoyment of God. Our bodies need no material refreshments as meat, drink, sleep, and raiment, which were the support of our bodies below.

The Prophet then said: "Have you not read that the Blessed Jesus, after His resurrection, appeared in His body to His disciples when they were met together in a chamber and the doors shut about them? Yet He called to Thomas to come and reach forth his hand and thrust it into His side. This shows it plainly to be substantial. The vision of our Blessed Lord is here what both our souls and bodies live upon and are supported by forever.

2. "Our bodies in the resurrection shall be immortal, and incapable of dying. Below their bodies are all mortal, dying, and perishing, and subject to be crumbled into dust every moment. Here our bodies will be incorruptible and freed from death forever. Our corruption here shall put on incorruption, and our mortality will be swallowed up in life."

God only has immortality

At this juncture, I desired the Prophet to bear with me a little, while I gave him an account of my own notions in this matter.

"Say on, for I am ready to remove your doubt," he said.

"I have learned," I said, "in the Holy Scriptures that immortality is an attribute that belongs to God only, and not to men, especially to the bodies of men, which every day's experience tells us are mortal. Therefore Paul tells Timothy that *God only hath immortality.*"

Bodies of deceased Saints still under death's power

The Prophet added: "When I say that bodies of the Blessed here are immortal, I intend it of bodies in their raised state. Then they are subject unto death no more. Man in his corruptible state is mortal and subject unto death. There is nothing more evident to all that dwell in the world below. Even the *bodies of all those Glorified Souls that are here are at this time kept under the power of death*.

"At the resurrection state when they shall be raised up again, they shall then be immortal. And as to what you urge from the Scripture, that only the Blessed God has immortality, it is very true. He is most eminently and essentially so; there is no creature, either Angel or man, that can, in that strict sense, be said to be so.

"We are immortal through His grace and favor. God is immortal in His essence and has been so from all eternity, and in that sense may well be said only to have immortality. Therefore it will not be amiss for you to observe that whatever the Blessed God is, He is essentially so. In which respect it is likewise said of Him that **He only is holy, and there is none good but God, none righteous, nor none merciful but He, to Whom be blessing, and glory, and honor, and praise forever and forevermore.**"

"I will give thee the treasures of darkness, and hidden riches of secret places . . . "
Isa. 45:3

Am I afraid to say that Holy Writ,
Which for its style and phrase puts down all wit,
Is everywhere so full of all these things,
(Dark figures, allegories), yet there springs
From that same book that lustre and those rays
Of light that turns our darkest nights to days.

John Bunyan

He that is down, needs fear no fall,
He that is low, no pride:
He that is humble, ever shall
Have God to be his guide.

John Bunyan

Chapter V

Imminence and Knowledge Differ

"O Holy Prophet," I remarked, "I saw among the many Blessed Souls I passed by as my Bright Messenger brought me to you, some that appeared to shine with greater brightness than the others. Are there among the Blessed different degrees of glory?"

Elijah replied, "The happiness and glory which all the Blessed here enjoy is the result of their communion with, and love for, the ever Blessed God, whose beautiful vision is the Eternal Spring from whence it flows. The more we see, the more we love. Love assimilates our souls into the nature of the blessed object of it; and thence results our glory. This makes a difference in the degrees of glory.

"Here there is no murmuring in one to see another's glory much greater than his own. The ever Blessed God is an unbounded ocean of light, and life, and joy, and happiness. It fills every vessel that is put therein till it can hold no more. And though the vessels are of several sizes, while each is filled, there is none that can complain.

"My answer therefore to your question is that those who have the most enlarged faculties do love God most, and are thereby assimilated most into His likeness. This is the highest glory Heaven can give. Nor let this seem strange to you, for even among God's Flaming Angels there are diversities of order and different degrees of glory. Perhaps these were some of those you saw as you came hither."

A "Redeemed One" comments

While I was thus talking with the Prophet, a shining form drew near. It was one of the Redeemed. He told me he had left his body below, resting in hope until the resurrection. And, that though he was still a substance, yet it was an immaterial one, not to be touched by mortal.

The Redeemed One said, "We here behold a sight worth dying for — the Blessed Lamb of God, the Glorious Saviour. Here we see Him in the regal state that belongs to Him by virtue of His kingly office, on account of which He is styled King of Kings and Lord of Lords. But, all the glorious greatness of our Blessed Redeemer does not make His kindness less familiar, but only more obliging. It makes Heaven more than Heaven to me to find Him reigning here, Who suffered so much for me in the world below."

Redeemed One continued, "Our Redeemer's happiness, which is so great and so ineffable, brings an increase to ours, according to the ardency of our love to Him. Here He invites each faithful servant to no less a blessing than to enter into His Master's joy."

We shall know each other

He added, "Here we see not only our elder Brother, Christ, but also our friends and relatives. Thus, though Elijah lived in the world below long before your time, *you no sooner saw him than you knew him*. And, so you will know Adam also when you see him. Here we communicate the purest pleasure to each other, an unfeigned ardent love uniting all our pure society.

"Here everyone is perfectly amiable and perfectly enamored with each other. And, oh, how happy is that state of love! How it doth ravish me to see my fellow Saints shining with an immortal loveliness! Where there is love like this, all needs must be delight. How can it be otherwise, since in this blessed society there is a continual receiving and returning of love and joy, and their conversation and intercourse is ravishing."

Earth's unknowable made known

"All the happiness that comes to us by knowledge of our friends and relatives, and that which comes from communion with God, and with each other is *above proclaiming*.

"However, it is to me a mighty happiness to understand all those deep and obscure mysteries of religion, which the profoundest Rabbis of the world below could not fully understand. Here we discern a *perfect harmony between those texts* that in the world below seemed most at variance. Here we are especially transported with wonder and gratitude at discoveries of the divine goodness towards each one of us in particular."

Sufferings made plain

"O Epenetus (Bunyan)! I have seen towards myself not only the *mercifulness* of those very afflictions that I once (when upon earth) imputed to *His severity*. I am fully convinced no stroke I met with in the world below (and I met with many, as well as great afflictions) either came *sooner or fell heavier or stood longer than was needful*. I am sure my hopes were never disappointed, but to secure my title to better things than what I hoped for."

A frail body grasps little

The Redeemed One, as offering an apology, said, "But I remember, Epenetus (Bunyan), you are still in the body, and may be tired with hearing what I could be forever telling. So vast is the happiness that I possess, and so great is the pleasure in telling it.

"I shall now add only one other thing concerning our happiness. The vast multitude of Blessed Souls who are partakers of this joy and glory does detract nothing from each private share. For this ocean of happiness is so bottomless that the innumerable company of all the Saints and Angels never can exhaust it.

"Think it not strange, for in the world below each nation does alike enjoy the benefit of light. Nor is there any that can complain he enjoys it less because another enjoys it also. All enjoy its benefit as fully as if none else enjoyed it but themselves. Indeed there is this difference between the Sun of Righteousness and that sun which shines upon the world below. Whereas the world's sun eclipses all the planets (his attendants), the Sun of Righteousness will, by His presence, impart splendor to His Saints.

"If a multitude of persons drink of the same river, none of them is able to exhaust it. Yet each of them has the full liberty of drinking as much as he can. So whoever enjoys God enjoys Him in relation to his capacity.

"Thus Epenetus (Bunyan), I have given you a brief account of our Celestial Canaan. It is *not the thousandth part* of that which might be said, yet it is enough to let you see it is a land flowing with milk and honey. And, it may well serve to whet your longing for a more experiential knowledge of it. For none can fully know the happiness we here enjoy until they come to be partakers of it.

"In this happy place worldly relations cease. Nor is there male and female here, but all are like the Angels, and therefore, all relations are here swallowed up in God."

Conductors change

Redeemed One had no sooner spoken, than taking me by the hand, far swifter than an arrow from a bow, we passed by several Shining Forms clothed in robes of immortality. They seemed to wonder at me as I passed them. He said to me, "Farewell, my Epenetus, (Bunyan), your Guardian Angel will be with you straightway, and reconduct you to the world below."

Feminine Escort

I drew near the shining form of another Redeemed One that stood before me. She appeared extremely glorious, compassed round with rays of dazzling luster. I hardly could behold her for the exceeding brightness of her face.

She said to me, "For what I am, to Him that is on the Throne be all the praise and glory. The robe of glory which you see me wear is only the reflection of His own bright beams!"

I said, "You speak like one who feels the mighty joys you are possessed of."

My feminine guide replied, "You should not think this strange. The mighty wonders of divine love and grace will be the subject of our song forever. Here all human relations cease and are all swallowed up in God. He is alone the great Father of all this heavenly family.

"Since I have put off the body, I have with that too put off all relations in the flesh. We are all children of one Father here, and servants of one Master. His blessed service is our perfect freedom."

About those on earth

She continued, "As for those I left behind me in the world below, I have committed them to God. I shall be glad to see them all heirs of this blessed inheritance. But, if they should close in with the *grand enemy of souls*, and refuse the grace offered them, and thereby perish in their unbelief, God will be glorified in His justice. And in His glory I shall still rejoice."

At this I was urged to know whether the Blessed understood what was going on in the world below, and whether they had any concern therein.

This Redeemed One replied. "As to the affairs of particular persons, *we are not concerned with them and are ignorant of them.* The being present in all places is an attribute peculiar to God alone. In His sight every creature is manifest. The prosperity or adversity of the Church below in their militant state is represented to us by the Angels. These are ministering spirits sent forth to minister to those that shall be heirs of salvation. And, from what we learn, we are excited to renew our praises to Him, that sits upon the throne!"

———————————

May I not write in such a style as this?
In such a method too, and yet not miss
Mine end, thy good? why may it not be done?
Dark clouds bring waters,
      when the bright bring none;

Yea, dark, or bright, if they their silver drops
Cause to descend, the earth by yielding crops
Gives praise to both, and carpeth not at either,
But treasures up the fruit they yield together:

      Excerpt of Apology to *Pilgrim's Progress*
          John Bunyan

When thou hast told the world of all these things,
Then turn about, my book, and touch these strings,
Which, if but touched will such music make,
They'll make a cripple dance, a giant quake.

John Bunyan

"Let us endeavor so to live
that when we come to die,
even the undertaker will be sorry."

Mark Twain

"There is no death! The stars go down to rise
upon some fairer shore."

J. L. McCreery

Christianity can be hazardous to your health.

"In Hell he lifted up his eyes,
being in torments . . . "

Jesus, Luke 16:23

Thou, Love Almighty, canst not make a hell,
Who doest all things well.
But rebel angel and malignant man
Together can.

Anonymous

Art thou forgetful? Wouldest thou remember
From New Year's Day to the last of December?
Then ponder my travels, they will stick like burrs,
And may be to the helpless, comforters.

This book is writ in such a dialect
As may the minds of listless men affect:
It is not a novelty, for it contains
Nothing but honest Gospel-strains.

John Bunyan

Chapter VI

Descent To Hell

This Redeemed One had no sooner spoken these things, and she departed. Instantly, the Bright Form that brought me from the world below into this place of happiness was present with me.

License to outer darkness

The Bright Form announced, "I have a commission to reconduct you to the world below; not only to the earth from whence I took you, but to the regions of the Prince of Darkness. There you will see the reward of sin, and what Justice has prepared as the just judgment of their rebellion, who would exalt themselves above the Throne of the Most High."

Fear not

"Do not therefore be afraid, for as I have a commission to take you thither, so have I likewise a mandate to bring you back again, and leave you in the world from whence I took you."

Leaving Heaven for earth was *extremely distasteful* and would have rendered me unhappy, but that I knew the *divine will* was such. But, to leave Heaven for Hell was that which turned my very heart within me.

However, when I knew that it was the divine good pleasure that I should be returned from thence to earth again, and there put off mortality, and then be reconducted up to Heaven, I was a little comforted. I found within myself an entire resignation to the will of God.

God's presence — in Hell

To my Bright Conductor, I said with some assurance, "That which the Blessed God has ordered I shall be always willing to obey. His great mercy I have already had so very large experience, that even in Hell itself I will not fear, may I but have His presence with me there."

To this my Shining Guardian answered me, "Wherever the Blessed God grants His presence, there is Heaven, and while we are in Hell, He will be with us."

Descent faster than thought

Bowing low before the Almighty's Throne, swifter than thought, my Guardian Angel carried me more than ten thousand leagues below the imperial heavens. When I saw those mighty globes of fire, those ever burning lamps of the ethereal heavens, I thus bespoke to my Bright Conductor that I had heard when I was upon earth that all of these fixed stars were worlds.

Star struck

I believed they might be. Here they are of such a mighty magnitude, but they seem to us on earth just such small things as what the earth seems here. "Please, may I be willingly informed from you what truth there is therein?"

My Shining Guardian answered me, "To Him who is almighty there is nothing impossible. Nor can there be a bound set to infinity. The ever Blessed God took six days' time to make the world below, but *could as well have made it in one moment* if He had so determined.

"It was the putting forth of His almighty power that did effect it. And, what that power can do, there is none can tell, but He that does possess it. But from His power, to argue it is His will, is no good logic in the School of Heaven. He does whatever He pleases, both in Heaven above and in the earth below. *What He pleases to reveal to us, we know; and what He has not so revealed, are secrets locked up in His own eternal counsel.*

"It is a bold and presumptuous curiosity for any creature to inquire into. There is no doubt but He can make as many worlds as there are stars in Heaven if it pleases Him. However, *if He has done so He has not yet revealed*, nor is it therefore our duty to inquire."

Inhabitants of "High Places" — despicable

By the time we reached the lowest regions of the air, I saw multitudes of *horrid forms and dismal dark appearances* fly from the shining presence of my Bright Conductor. "These sure," said I, "are some of the Vanguard of Hell, so black and so affrighting are their forms."

"These are," said my Conductor, "some of the Apostate Spirits that wander up and down *in the air and on earth* like roaring lions seeking whom they may devour. Though they are led hence, you will see them quickly in their own dark territories, for we are now upon the borders of the infernal pit."

Oh! eyes! nose! ears!

Quick as a wink, I found the words of my Conductor very true. We were soon surrounded with a *darkness much more black than night*. It was attended with a *stink more suffocating far than that of burning brimstone*. My ears were likewise filled *with horrid yellings of the damned spirits*. All the most discordant notes on earth were, in comparison of this, melodious music.

"Now," said my Guardian Angel, "you are on the verge of Hell. Do not fear the power of the Destroyer. My commission from the Imperial Throne secures you from all dangers!"

Question & Answer Session

"Here it is your permit to hear from Devils and Damned Souls the cursed causes of their endless ruin. And, what you have a mind to ask, **inquire**! They shall answer you! The Devils cannot hurt you, though they would. They are bound by Him that has commissioned me, *of which themselves are cog-*

nizant. For such cause, this makes them rage and fret and roar and bite their hated chains, but all in vain."

We now were come within Hell's territories, placed in the caverns of the infernal deep. There earth's center reconciles all things, where all effects do in their causes sleep. There, in a sulphurous lake of liquid fire, bound with the chain of Heaven's fixed decree, sat Lucifer upon a Burning Throne. His horrid eyes were sparkling with hellish fury — as full of rage as his strong pains could make him.

"Intelligence" at work

Those wandering fiends, that as we came from Heaven fled before us, had (I perceived) been given notice of our coming. *This put all Hell in an uproar*. It made Lucifer to vent his horrid blasphemies against the Blessed God, which he delivered with an air of arrogance and pride.

Lucifer's rage

Hell's Chief roared, "What would the Thunderer have? He has my Heaven already! His radiant scepter this bold hand should bear! And for those never fading fields of light — my fair inheritance — I am confined here in this dark house of death, sorrow, and woe! What, would He have Hell from me too that He insults me here?

"Ah! Could I but obtain another day to try it in. I would make Heaven shake and His Bright Throne to totter. Nor would I fear the utmost of His power, though He had fiercer flames than these to throw me in. If then I lost the day, the fault was not mine! *No winged spirit in Heaven's arched roof bid fairer for the victory than I did*!"

Wrath toward God turned on man

With a changed voice, he continued, "But, ah! that day is lost. I am doomed, forever doomed, to these dark territories! But, it is at least some comfort to me still that *mankind's sorrow waits upon my woe!* And, since I cannot on the Thunderer, I will wreak the utmost of my rage on them."

I was amazed to hear his impious speech, and could not forbear saying to my Conductor, "How justly are his blasphemies rewarded!"

The Angel replied, "What you have heard from this Apostate Spirit is both his sin and punishment; for every blasphemy he belches against Heaven makes Hell the hotter to him."

Friends in Hell

We then passed on further, among dismal scenes of unmixed sorrow. We saw two Wretched Souls tormented by a Fiend, who without ceasing, plunged them in liquid fire and burning brimstone. They, at the same time, accused and cursed each other.

One of them said to his tormented fellow sufferer, "O cursed be your face, that ever I set eyes upon you! My misery is due to you. I may thank you for this, for it was your persuasions that brought me hither. You enticed me; you it was who ensnared me thus. It was your covetousness and cheating and your oppression and grinding of the poor that brought me hither.

"Ah, if you had but set me a good example as you did an ill one, I might have been in Heaven. There I would have been as happy as I am now miserable. But O Wretch that I was, my following your steps has made me in this wretched state and ruined me forever! O that I never had seen your face, or you had never been born to do my soul that wrong that you have done."

The other Wretch replied, "And may I not as well blame you? For do you not remember how at such a time and place you did entice me and drew me out and asked me if I would not go along with you? I was about my other business, about my lawful calling! But you called me away, and therefore are as much in fault as I.

"Though I was covetous, yet you were proud. If you learned of me your covetousness, I am sure I learned of you my pride and drunkenness. Though you learned of me to cheat, yet you taught me to lust, to lie, and scoff at goodness.

"Thus, though I stumbled you in some things, you stumbled me as much in others. Therefore, if you blame me, I can blame you as much. If I have to answer for some of your most filthy actions, you have still to answer for some of mine. I wish you never had come hither. The very looks of you do wound my soul by bringing sin afresh into my mind.

"So, it was with you, with you it was I sinned. O grief unto my soul! And since I could not shun your company there, *O that I could have been without it here!*"

From this sad dialogue I soon perceived that those who are companions upon earth in sin shall be so too in Hell in punishment. Though on earth they love each other's company, they will not care for it in Hell.

This, I believe, was the true reason why Dives (the Rich Man) seemed so charitable to his brethren, that they might not come into his place of torment. It was love unto himself, and not to them, that was his motive. Because, had they come thither, his torments would have thereby been increased.

The furnace

"The Son of man shall send forth His angels, and they shall gather out of His kingdom all things that offend, and them which do iniquity;

"And shall cast them into a furnace of fire: there shall be wailing and gnashing of teeth.

*"Then shall the **righteous shine forth as the sun**."*

Jesus, Mat. 13:41-43

YOU have laughed God out of your schools,
out of your books, and out of your life,
but you cannot laugh Him
out of your death.

Dagobert Runes

After a 12 year imprisonment without a trial, replying to the question, "If released, will you agree to quit preaching?" Bunyan answered:

"I am determined, Almighty God being my helper, yet to suffer, if frail life might continue, even till moss shall grow over my eyebrows, rather than violate my faith and butcher my conscience."

John Bunyan

Chapter VII

Feats of the Doomed

There were yet more tragic scenes of sorrow. Leaving these two cursed wretches, accusing each other for being authors of each other's misery, we passed on further, beholding several woeful spectacles.

One of these I will relate. There was one who had flaming sulphur forced down her throat by a tormenting spirit. He did this with such horrid cruelty and insolence, I could not but say to him, "Why should you so delight in the tormenting of that cursed wretch as to be thus perpetually pouring that flaming, infernal liquor down her throat?"

For the love of money?

The Fiend replied, "This is no more but a just retribution. This woman in her lifetime was such a sordid wretch that though she had gold enough, she could never be satisfied. Therefore now I pour it down her throat. She cared not who she ruined and undid so she could get their gold.

"When she had amassed together a greater treasure than ever she could spend, her love of money would not let her spend so much of it as to supply herself with what the common necessities of life required. She then went often with an empty stomach, though her bags were full, or else she filled it at another's charge.

"As for her apparel, it either never grew old, or it was always so supplied with patches that at last it was hard to say which piece was an original.

"She kept no house because she would not be taxed. She kept her treasure in her hands for fear she should be robbed. She would not let it out on bonds and mortgages for fear of being cheated, although she ever cheated all she could. She was herself so great a cheat, that she cheated her own body of its food and her own soul of mercy. Since gold then was her god on earth, is it not just that she should have her belly full in Hell?"

The damned still lie

When her tormentor had done speaking, I asked her whether what he said was true or not. To this she answered me, "No, to my grief it is not." "How! to your grief?" said I.

Entice Heaven?

"Yes, to my grief," said she. "Because were that which my tormentor tells you true, I should be better satisfied. He tells you that it is gold that he pours down my throat, but he is a lying devil and speaks falsely.

"Were it but gold I never should complain. But he abuses me, and in the stead of gold he only gives the horrid, stinking sulphur. Had I my gold I should be happy still. I so truly value it, that if I had it here, I scarce would *bribe Heaven* with it to be removed thence."

I could not forbear telling my Conductor I was amazed to hear a wretch in Hell itself so to dote upon her riches and that, too, while in the tormentor's hands!

My Conductor said, "This may convince you it is sin that is the greatest of all evils. It is the greatest of all punishments to be abandoned to the love of sin. The love of gold (to which this cursed creature is given up), is a more fatal punishment than that which the Apostate Spirits here inflict upon her."

"O!" said I, "could but wicked men on earth, for one small moment lay their ears to this mouth of Hell and hear those horrid shrieks of damned souls, they could not be in love with sin again."

Corrected

"Eternal Truth has told us otherwise. Those who will not fear His Ministers, nor have regard to what His Word contains, will not be warned **though one should come from Hell**."

Let me hear on

We had not come much farther before we saw a wretched soul lying on a bed of burning steel. Almost choked with brimstone, he cried out as one under a dreadful anguish, with a note of desperation. This made me desire of my Conductor to stay awhile that I might listen more attentively to what he said. Hereupon I heard him speak as follows:

"Ah, miserable Wretch! Undone forever, forever! Oh, these killing words, **forever**! Will not a thousand, thousand years suffice to bear that pain?

could avoid it, I would not bear one moment for a thousand, thousand worlds?

"No, no, my misery never will have an end. After the thousand thousand years it will be **forever** still. Oh, hapless, helpless, hopeless state indeed! It is this forever that is the Hell of Hell!"

Thousands of opportunities

"O cursed Wretch! Cursed to all eternity! How willfully have I undone myself! Oh, what stupendous folly am I guilty of to choose sin's short and momentary pleasure at the dear price of everlasting pain! How oft have I been told it would be so! How often pressed to leave those paths of sin that would be sure to bring me to the chambers of eternal death!

"Yet I might once have helped all this, and would not! Oh, that is the gnawing worm that never dies! I might once have been happy. Salvation once was offered me, and I refused it. Ah, had it been but once! Yet to refuse it had been a folly not to be forgiven, *for it was offered me a thousand times*! But (wretch that I was) I still as often refused it.

"O cursed sin, that with deluding pleasures bewitches mankind to eternal ruin! *God often called, but I as often refused. He stretched His hand out, but I would not mind it. How often have I set at nought His counsel! How often have I refused His reproof!*

81

"How the scene is changed. The case is altered. Now He laughs at my calamity and mocks at the destruction which is come upon me. He would have helped me once, but then I would not. Therefore those eternal miseries I am condemned to undergo are but the just reward of my own doing."

Somber sentiments

I could not hear this doleful lamentation without reflecting on the *wondrous* grace that ever Blessed God has shown to me. Eternal praises to His holy name! For my heart told me that I had deserved as much as that sad Wretch to be the object of eternal wrath. It is His grace alone, that has made us differ!

O how unsearchable His counsels be!
And who can fathom His divine decree?

Sympathy without remedy

After these reflections I addressed myself to the Doleful Complainer. I told him I had heard his woeful lamentation. I perceived his misery was great and his loss irreparable. I told him I would willingly be informed of it more particularly, which might possibly be some lessening of his sufferings.

He responded, "No, not at all. My pains are such as can admit of no relief, no, not for one small moment. But by the question you have asked, I do perceive you are a stranger here, and **may you ever be so**. Ah! had I but the least hopes still remaining, how would I kneel and cry and pray forever to be redeemed from hence! But ah! it is all in vain. I am lost forever. That you may beware of coming hither, I will tell you what the damned suffer here."

To move me for to watch and pray,
To strive to be sincere,
To take my Cross up day by day,
And serve the Lord with fear.

John Bunyan

In Bedford Jail

"The parting with my wife and poor children has often been to me in this place as pulling flesh from the bones . . . And oh! my poor blind child lay nearer to my heart than all the others . . . Poor child, what sorrow you are likely to have for your portion. You must beg, be beaten, suffer hunger, cold, nakedness and a thousand calamities, though I cannot now endure that the wind should blow upon you . . .

"Yet I must entrust you all with God, though it goes to the quick to leave you. However, three considerations are warm upon my heart:

> 1.   "I thought on those two milk cows that were to carry the ark of God into another country, and to leave their calves behind them; I Sam. 6:10.

> 2.   "Leave thy fatherless children, I will preserve them alive; and let thy widows trust in me," Jer. 49:11.

> 3.   "The Lord said, Verily it shall be well with thy remnant; verily I will cause the enemy to entreat thee well in the time of evil . . ." Jer. 15:11.

John Bunyan
Autobiography

Chapter VIII

Classification of Torments

This Doleful Complainer seemed eager to continue enlightening me on the depths of despair experienced by Hell's inhabitants. He proceeded:

"Our miseries in this infernal dungeon are of two sorts —

* What we have lost, and
* What we undergo.

His presence — fulness of joy

1. "In this sad, dark abode of misery and sorrow, we have lost the presence of the ever Blessed God. This is that which makes this dungeon Hell. Though

we had lost a thousand worlds, it would not be so much as this one loss. Could but the least glimpse of His favor enter here, we might be happy, but we have lost it to our everlasting woe.

2. "Here we have likewise lost the company of Saints and Angels. In their place we have nothing but tormenting Devils.

3. "Here we have lost Heaven, too, the seat of blessedness. There is a deep gulf betwixt us and Heaven, so that we are shut out from thence forever. Those Everlasting Gates that let the Blessed into happiness are now forever shut against us here.

4. "To make our wretchedness far yet more wretched, we have lost the hope of ever being in a better state, which renders our condition truly hopeless. The most miserable man upon earth still has hope. And therefore, it is a common proverb there that were it not for hope, the heart would break.

"Well may our hearts break then, since we are both without hope and help. This is what we have lost. To think on, is enough to fear and rend and gnaw upon our miserable souls forever. Yet, oh, that this were all! But we have **sense of pain** as well as **loss**. And having showed you what we have lost, I will now try to show you what we undergo."

What we endure

1. "First, we undergo a variety of torments. We are tormented here a thousand, nay, ten thousand different ways. They that are most afflicted upon earth have seldom any more than one malady at a time. But should they have the plague, the gout, the stone, and fever at one time, how miserable would they think themselves?"

Fire and darkness

"Yet all those are but like the biting of a flea to those intolerable, pungent pains that we endure. Here we have all the loathed variety of Hell to grapple with. Here is a fire that is **unquenchable to burn us with**, a lake of burning brimstone **ever choking us**, and **eternal chains** to tie us. Here is utter **darkness to affright us** and a worm of conscience that gnaws upon us everlastingly. Any one of these is worse to bear than all the torments mankind ever felt on earth."

Each body part punished

2. "As our torments here are various, so are they universal, afflicting each part of the body and

tormenting all the powers of the soul, which render what we suffer most unsufferable. In those illnesses you are seized with on earth, though some parts are afflicted, other parts are free. Although your body may be out of order, your head may yet be well. Though your head be ill, your vitals may be free. Though your vitals be affected, your arms and legs may still be clear. But here it is otherwise. Each member of the soul and body is at once tormented.

* "The *eye* is here tormented with the sight of devils who do appear in all the horrid shapes and black appearances that sin can give them.

* "The *ear* is continually tormented with the loud yellings and continual out-cries of the damned.

* "The *nostrils* are smothered with sul-phurous flames.

* "The *tongue* burns with fiery blisters.

* "The *whole body* is rolled in flames of liquid fire.

"All the powers and faculties of our souls are here tormented. Ever present are the imagination with the thoughts of present pain, the memory re-flecting on what a heaven we have lost, and of those opportunities we had of being saved.

"Our minds are here tormented with considering how vainly we have spent our precious time and how we have abused it. Our understanding is tormented in the thoughts of our past pleasures, present pains, and future sorrows, which are to last forever. Our consciences are tormented with a continual gnawing worm."

Outer limits of endurance

3. "Another thing that makes our misery awful is the **extremity of our torments**. The fire that burns us is so violent that all the water in the sea can never quench it. The pains we suffer here are so extreme that it is impossible they should be known by anyone but those that feel them.

4. "Another part of our misery is the **ceaseless-ness of our torments**. As various, as universal, and as extremely violent as they are, they are continual, too. Nor have we the least rest from them. If there were any relaxation, it might be some allay. This makes our condition so deplorable that there is no easing of our torments, but what we suffer now we must forever suffer.

Misery that doesn't love company

5. "The **society of company** we have here is another element in our misery. Tormenting devils

and tormented souls are all our company. Dreadful shrieks and howlings, under the fierceness of our pain, and fearful oaths, is all our conversation. Here the torments of our Fellow Sufferers are so far from lessening our misery that they increase our pain.

6. "**The place** in which we suffer is another thing that increases our sufferings. It is the abstract of all misery — a prison, a dungeon, a bottomless pit, a lake of fire and brimstone, a furnace of fire that burns to eternity, the blackness of darkness forever, and lastly, Hell itself. Such a wretched place as this must needs increase our wretchedness.

7. "**The cruelty of our tormentors** is another thing that adds to our torments. Our tormentors are devils in whom there is no pity; being tormented themselves, they do yet take pleasure in tormenting us.

8. "All those particulars that I have reckoned up are very grievous, but that which makes them much more grievous is that they shall ever be so. All our most intolerable sufferings shall last to all eternity. 'Depart from me ye cursed into everlasting fire' is that which is perpetually sounding in my ears! Oh, that I could reverse that fatal sentence! Oh, that there was but a bare possibility of doing it! Thus have I showed you the miserable situation we are in and shall be in forever."

For those that were not for my little book,
I said to them, offend you I am loth;
Yet since your brethren pleased with it be,
Forbear to judge, till you do further see.
If that thou wilt not read, let it alone;
Some love the meat, some love to pick the bone:

John Bunyan

The Prince of Darkness grim,
We tremble not for him;
His rage we can endure.
For lo! his doom is sure.
One little word shall fell him.

But still our ancient foe,
Doth seem to work us woe;
His craft and power are great,
And armed with cruel hate,
On earth is not his equal.

Let goods and kindred go.
This mortal life also;
The body they may kill,
God's truth abideth still,
His Kingdom is forever.

Martin Luther, 1483-1546

"For Thy sake we are killed all the day long; we are counted as sheep for the slaughter," Rom. 8:36.

Chapter IX

Hell — Home of Deluded

This wretched soul had scarcely made an end of what he was saying before he was afresh tormented by a Hellish Fury, who bid him cease complaining, for it was in vain. "Besides," said he, "do you know you have deserved it?"

This Special Persecutor railed on relentlessly, "How often were you told of this before, but would not then believe it? You laughed at them that told you of a Hell. Nay, you were so presumptuous to dare Almighty justice to destroy you! How often have you called on God to damn you. Do you complain that now you are answered according to your wishes? What an unreasonable thing is this, that you should call so often for damnation and yet be so uneasy under it?"

You chose this, I didn't

The Fiend continued, "You know yourself you had salvation offered you and you refused it! With what face then can you complain of being damned? I have more reason to complain than you, for you have had a long time of repentance given you, but I was turned to Hell as soon as I had sinned.

"Remember, you had salvation offered you, and pardon and forgiveness often tendered you. I never had any mercy offered me, but was consigned as soon as I had sinned to everlasting punishment. If I had had the offer of salvation I never would have slighted it as you have done. It had been better for you that you had never had the offer of it either, for then damnation had been easier to you. Who do you think should pity you that would be damned in spite of Heaven itself?"

This made the Wretch cry out, "Oh, do not thus continue to torment me! I know that my destruction is of myself. Oh, that I could forget it! The thoughts of that is here **my greatest plague**. I would be damned, and therefore justly I am so."

Devil's beef

Then turning to the Fiend that tortured him, he said, "But it was through **thy temptations**, cursed Devil. It was thou that **tempted me** to all the sins I have been guilty of, and dost thou now upbraid me?

**You say you never had a Saviour offered you, but
you should call to mind you never had a tempter
either**, as I have had continually of thee."

You heard the truth

To this the Devil scornfully replied, "I own it was
my business to decoy you hither, and you have often
been told so by your preachers. They told you
plainly enough we sought your ruin and went about
continually like roaring lions seeking whom we
could devour. I was oft afraid you would believe
them, as several did, to our great disappointment.
But you were willing to do what we would have you,
and since you have done our work, it is but reason-
able that we should pay you wages."

Suddenly the Persecutor began a fresh torture.
This roar out was so horrible, I could no longer stay
to hear him, and so passed on.

I turned to my Conductor and said, "How dismal
these damned souls! They are the devil's slaves
while upon earth, and he upbraids and then torments
them for it when they come to Hell."

"Their malice against all the race of Adam," said
my Conductor, "is exceeding great. And because
many souls are ignorant of their devices, they easily
prevail upon them to their eternal ruin. How they
treat them here for listening to their temptations, you
have seen already and will see more of quickly."

Hell — hard on hypocrites

Passing a little further we saw a multitude of Damned Souls together, gnashing their teeth with extreme rage and pain. All the while the tormenting Fiends with hellish fury poured liquid fire and brimstone continually upon them. They, in the meantime, cursed God themselves, and those about them, in blaspheming after a tremendous manner. I could not forbear asking of one Fiend that so tormented them who they were that he used so cruelly.

Said the Torturer, "These are they that very well deserve it. These are those cursed wretches that would teach others the **right road** to Heaven while yet themselves were **so in love with Hell** that they came hither. These are those souls that have been the great factors of Hell upon the earth. Therefore, they deserve a particular regard in Hell.

"Here we use our utmost diligence to give everyone his utmost share of torments, but are sure to take care **these shall not want**. These have not only their own sins to answer for, but all those, too, whom they have led astray both by their doctrine and example."

Addressing myself to this Distressor, I said, "Since they have been such great factors for Hell, as you say, methinks gratitude should oblige you to use them a little more kindly."

No friendship there

The impudent Fiend answered me in a scoffing manner, "They that expect gratitude among devils will find themselves mistaken. Gratitude is a virtue, but we hate all virtue and profess an immortal enmity against it.

"Besides, we hate all mankind, and were it in our power, not one of them should be happy. It is true we do not tell them so upon earth. There it is our business to flatter and delude them. But, when we have them here where they are fast enough (for from Hell there is no redemption), we soon convince them of their folly in believing us."

Heaven — unmerited

From the discourse I had heard of this and other of the devils, I could not but reflect that it is **infinite and unspeakable grace** by which any poor sinners are brought to Heaven! How many snares and baits are laid by the enemy of souls to entrap them by the way!

Therefore it is a work well worthy of the Blessed Son of God to save His people from their sins, and to deliver them from the wrath to come. It is an unaccountable folly and madness in men to refuse the offers of His grace and to close in with the Destroyer.

Deathbed deception

Journeying on in this vast region, my Conductor by my side, I heard a Wretch complaining in a heartbreaking strain against those men that had betrayed him hither.

"I was told," said he, "by those that I depended on and thought could have informed me right, that if I said but 'Lord, have mercy on me' when I came to die, it would be enough to save me. But, oh, wretchedly I find myself mistaken, to my eternal sorrow! Alas, I called for mercy on my deathbed, but found it was too late. This Cursed Devil here that told me just before that I was safe enough, then told me it was **too late**; and Hell must be my portion."

Devils can preach

"You see I told you true at last," said the Devil, "and then you would not believe me. A very pretty business, is it not, think you? You spend your days in the pursuit of sin, and wallow in your filthiness, and you would go to Heaven when you die!"

The Devil said on, "Would any but a madman think that would ever do? No. He that in good earnest does intend to go to Heaven when he dies must walk in **ways of holiness and virtue** while he lives. You say some of your lewd companions told you that saying 'Lord, have mercy on me' when you came to die would be enough. A very fine excuse!

"You might have known if you'd have given yourself but leisure to read the Bible that '**without holiness none shall see the Lord**.' Therefore this is the sum of the matter. You were willing to live in your sins as long as you could. You did not leave them at last because you did not like them, but because you could follow them no longer. This you know to be true."

The sermonizing Devil added, "Could you have the impudence to think to go to Heaven with the love of sin in your heart? No, no, no such matter. You have been warned often enough that you should take heed of being deceived. **God is not mocked.** Such as you sowed, you would also reap. You have no reason to complain of anything but your own folly, which you now see too late."

To my Conductor, I said, "This lecture of the Devil was a very cutting one to the poor tormented Wretch. Alas, it contains the true case of many now on earth, as well as those in Hell. But, oh, what a far different judgment do they make in this sad state from what they did on earth."

"The reason for this is," replied my Guardian Angel, "that they will not allow themselves to think what the effect of sin will be, nor what an evil it is, while upon earth. It is **in consideration** that is the ruin of so many thousands, who think not what they are doing, nor where they are going, until it is too late to help it."

One may live as a conqueror,
a king, or a magistrate;
but he must die as a man.

Daniel Webster

What danger is the pilgrim in,
How many are his foes,
How many ways there are to sin,
No living mortal knows.
Some of the ditch shy are, yet can
Lie tumbling in the mire:
Some though they shun the frying-pan,
Do leap into the fire.

John Bunyan

Put by the curtains, look within my veil
Turn up the lamp, and do not fail:
There if thou seekest them such things to find
As will be helpful to an honest mind.

John Bunyan

Chapter X

No Atheists in Hell

We were traveling on in this pit of darkness and soon heard another tormenting himself and increasing his own misery by thinking of the happiness of the Blessed Souls in Heaven.

We were diverted from giving any further ear unto these stinging self-reflections of this poor Lost Creature. We approached a vast number of tormenting Fiends lashing incessantly a numerous company of wretched souls with knotted whips of ever burning steel. They roared out with cries so very piercing and so lamentable I thought it might have melted even cruelty itself into some pity.

Such made me say to one of the Tormentors, "Oh, stay your hand, and do not use such cruelty as this to them who are your **fellow creatures**, and whom perhaps you have yourselves betrayed to all this misery."

Unusual chastening reserved for Atheists

The Tormentor answered very smoothly, "No, though we are bad enough, no Devil ever was as bad as they, nor guilty of such crimes as they have been. For **we all know there is a God**, although we hate Him; but these are such as never could be brought to own (till they came hither) **that there was such a Being**."

"Then these," said I, "are Atheists, wretched sort of men indeed, and who once wanted to ruin me, had not eternal grace prevented it."

Bunyan recognized by "old friend"

I had no sooner spoken, but one of the Tormented Wretches   cried out with a sad mournful accent, "Sure, I should know that voice. It must be Epenetus (Bunyan)."

I was amazed to hear my name mentioned by one of the infernal crew. Being desirous to know what it was, I answered, "Yes, I am Epenetus (Bunyan), but who are you in that sad lost condition that knows me? To this the lost unknown replied, "I was once well acquainted with you upon earth and had almost persuaded you to be of my opinion. I am the author of that celebrated book by the title *Leviathan*."

"What! the great Hobbs?" said I. "Are you come hither? Your voice is so much changed I did not know it."

"Alas," replied he, "I am that unhappy man indeed. But am so far from being great that I am one of the **most wretched** persons in all these sooty territories. Nor is it any wonder that my voice is changed; for I am now changed in my principles, though changed too late to do me any good.

"Now I know there is a God. But, oh, I wish there were not, for I am sure He will have no mercy on me. Nor is there any reason that He should. I do confess I was His foe on earth, and now He is mine in Hell. It is that wretched confidence I had in my own wisdom that has thus betrayed me."

I admitted, "Your case is miserable, and yet you needs must own you suffer justly. For how **industrious** were you to persuade others, and so involve them in the same damnation. None has more reason to know this than I, who had almost been taken in the snare and perished forever."

The former Atheist replied, "It stings me to the heart, to think how many perish by my means. I was afraid when first I heard your voice that you had likewise been **consigned to punishment**. Not that I can wish any person happy, for it is my plague to think that any are so, while I am miserable. But, every soul that is brought hither, through my seduction while I was on earth, doubles my pains in Hell!

An Atheist, really?

"Oh, tell me, for I fain would be informed, and you can do it. Did you indeed believe when upon earth that **there was no God**? Could you imagine that the world could make itself and that the creatures were the causes of their own production? Had you no **secret whispers** in your soul that told you it was another made you and not you yourself? Had you never any doubts about this matter?

"I have often heard it said that though there are many who profess there is no God, there is not one that thinks so. It would be strange there should, because there is none, but carry in their bosom a witness for that God whom they deny. Now you can tell whether it is so or no, and you have now no reason to conceal your sentiments."

He answered me, "Nor will I, although the thoughts thereof sting me afresh. I did at first believe there was a God. Then I fell afterwards to vicious courses, which rendered me open to His wrath. I then had some secret wishes there was none. It is impossible to think there is a God, and not withal to think Him just and righteous. Consequently, He is obliged to punish the transgressors of His law. Being I was conscious of myself as obnoxious to His justice, it made me hate Him and wish that there was no such being.

"Still pursuing the same vicious courses, and finding **justice did not overtake me**, I then began to hope there was no God. From those hopes began to frame in my own breast ideas suitable to what I hoped. Having thus in my own thoughts framed a new system of the world's origin, excluding the being of a Deity, I found myself so fond of these new notions, that I at last prevailed upon myself to give them credit. Then I endeavored to fasten the belief of them on others."

Had qualms

"Before I came to such a height as this, I do acknowledge that I found **several checks** in my own conscience for what I did. All along I was now and then troubled with some strange uneasy thoughts, as if I should not find all right at last, which I endeavored to put off, as much as in me lay.

"Now, I find those **checking thoughts** that might have been of service to me then, are here the things that most of all torment me. I must own the love of sin hardened my heart against my Maker and made me hate Him first, and then deny His being. Sin, that I hugged so close within my bosom, has been the cursed cause of all this woe; the serpent that has stung my soul to death.

"Now I find, in spite of my vain philosophy, there is a God. I find, too, now, that God will not be mocked, although it was my daily practice in the world to mock at Heaven and ridicule whatever things are sacred.

"These were the means I used to spread abroad my cursed notions, and which I always found very successful. For those I could get to ridicule the Sacred Oracles, I always looked upon to be in a fair way my disciples. Now, the thoughts thereof are more tormenting to me than all the torments I sustain by whip of burning steel."

"Beware lest any man spoil you through philosophy and vain deceit, after the tradition of men, after the rudiments of the world, and not *after Christ.*

For in Him dwelleth all the fulness of the Godhead bodily . . . In whom are hid all the treasures of wisdom and knowledge," Col. 2:8,9,3.

He first by grace must conquered be,
That sin would mortify.
And who that live would convince me,
Unto himself must die.

John Bunyan

The Lord is only my support,
And He that doth me feed:
How can I then want any thing
Whereof I stand in need?

John Bunyan

When at the first I took my pen in hand,
Thus for to write, I did not understand
That I at all should make a little book
In such a mode; nay, I had undertook
To make another, which when almost done,
Before I was aware, I this begun . . .

Thus I set pen to paper with delight,
And quickly had my thoughts in black and white.
For having now my method by the end,
Still as I pulled it came, and so I penned
It down, until it came at last to be
For length and breadth the bigness which you see.

Excerpt of Apology for *Pilgrim's Progress*
John Bunyan

Chapter XI

Fire, yet Darkness

To my former friend I must inquire another question. In these regions, I heard yourself and others cry out of burning steel and fire and flames. Yet I cannot discern it. Where there is fire, there must be some degree of light. But from what appears to me, you are still in utter darkness.

He answered me, "O that I could but say I felt no fire! How easy would my torments be to that which I now find them! But alas, the fire that we endure ten thousand times exceeds all culinary fire in fierceness and is of quite a different nature from it. **No light at all attends it**, as does fire as burns upon earth. But, notwithstanding, with all the fire in Hell, we are still in utter darkness.

Ever burning, never consuming!

Now he further explains the mystery, "The fire you burn on earth is of a preying and devouring nature. Whatsoever it takes hold of, it consumes to ashes. When it meets with no more fuel, it goes out. Here it is not so! Though it burns with that tremendous fierceness, which none but those that feel it know, yet does it not consume, nor ever will. We shall ever be burning, yet not burned up.

"This is a tormenting, but not a consuming fire. Here the fire seizes upon our souls and puts them into pain, so tormenting as cannot be expressed. It was my ignorance of this, when upon earth, that made me ridicule the notion of immaterial substances being burned by fire. Here, to my own cost, I find too true."

Hell fire uncontrolled

"Another difference betwixt the fire that burns us here and that which burns on earth, is this, that you can kindle that whenever you please and quench it when you will. Here it is otherwise. This fire is like to a stream of brimstone, and it burns forever. This is what I have to answer to the last sad question that you asked me."

"Sad indeed," said I. "See what Almighty Power can inflict on those that violate His righteous law."

Devil challenges Angel

The Apostate Spirit worms in his reply, "Why dost thou thus invade our territories and come here to torment us before our time?"

When this Persecutor had thus spoken, he slunk away, as if he durst not stay to have an answer.

Unanswered inquiry

Upon this Fiend's departure, I said to my Conductor, "Something I have heard about the fall of the Apostate Angels, but I have a great desire to be informed in the particulars thereof more fully." To this my Guardian Angel answered me, "When thou shalt once have put off thy mortality and be translated to the Blessed Abode, there thou shalt know such things as now thou canst not apprehend."

He continued, "Therefore in thy present state desire not to be wise above what is written. It is enough to know the Angels sinned, and for their sin were cast down to Hell. But how pure spirits should have a thought to arise in their hearts against the eternal Purity that first created them, is what thou art not capable of comprehending now."

Changing my emphasis, I said, "I have observed that all of these Wretched Ones complain most of the torment that arises from their own sense of guilt, which justifies the justice of the punishment. This gloomy prison is the **best glass** to behold sin in its most proper colors. Were there not the greatest malignity in sin, it would not be rewarded with so extreme a punishment."

Jesus Paid It All

My Guardian Angel said, "Your inference is very natural, but there is yet a better glass than this to see the just demerits due to sin. That is by contemplation to behold the Blessed Son of God upon the Cross. There we may see the dire effects of sin. There we may see its true malignity. For all the sufferings of the damned here are but the sufferings of creatures still, but on the cross you see a Suffering God."

Looking on the lost!

"For as the new heavens and the new earth, which I will make, shall remain before me, saith the LORD, so shall your seed and your name remain.

"And it shall come to pass, that from one new moon to another; and from one sabbath to another, shall all flesh come to worship before me, saith the LORD.

"And they shall go forth, and **look upon the carcases of the men that have transgressed against me: for their worm shall not die, neither shall their fire be quenched**; and they shall be an abhorring unto all flesh."

Isa. 66:22-24.

Family Prayer

Let the most Blessed be my guide,
If't be his blessed will,
Unto his Gate, into his fold,
Up to his Holy Hill.

And let him never suffer me
To swerve, or turn aside
From his free grace, and holy ways,
What e'er shall me betide.

And let him gather them of mine,
That I have left behind,
Lord make them pray they may be thine,
With all their heart and mind.

John Bunyan

Well Faithful, thou hast faithfully professed
Unto thy Lord: with him thou shalt be blest;
When faithless ones with all their vain delights
Are crying out under their hellish plights,
Sing, Faithful, sing, and let thy name survive,
For though they killed thee, thou art yet alive.

John Bunyan

Chapter XII

The Tempted —
in Heaven and Earth

While I was making some further observations on what I heard, the Relentless Fiend who was before tormenting them, thus interrupted me.

"You see by him what sort of men they were when in the world, and do you not think that they deserve the punishment they undergo?"

I answered, "Doubtless it is the just reward of sin which now they suffer, and which hereafter you shall suffer, too. You, as well as they, have sinned against the ever Blessed God, and for your sin shall suffer the just vengeance of eternal fire."

And further I added, "Nor is it in the least any excuse to say you never doubted the being of a God. For though you knew there was a God, yet you rebelled against Him. Therefore, you shall be justly punished with everlasting destruction from the presence of the Lord and from the glory of His power."

Man tempted by devils
Devils tempted by Satan

The Persecutor, attempting to justify himself, continues, "It is true we know we shall be punished as thou has said. However, if it be a reason why mankind should have pity showed them, because they fell through the temptations of the Devil, it is the same case with me and all the rest of the Inferior Spirits. For we were tempted by the **Bright Sun of the Morning** to take part with him. Therefore, though this aggravates the crime of Lucifer, it should extenuate that of Inferior Spirits."

My Guardian Angel counters

My Bright Conductor, who had not spoken to the Fallen Angels since my coming thither, thus replied with a stern, angry countenance: "O thou Apostate, Wicked, Lying Spirit! Canst thou affirm those things and see me here? Dost thou not know it was thy proud heart made thee take part with Lucifer against the Blessed God who had created thee a glorious creature?

"Thou knowest that thou didst pride thyself of thy own beauty, and wouldst have been above thy Blessed Creator, and so wert ready to take part with Lucifer. Justly art thou with him cast down to Hell. And, thy former comeliness and beauty are changed to that horrid monstrous form in which thou now appearest, as the just punishment of thy rebellious pride."

I replied, "Surely, justice and mercy did never so triumph and kiss each other as in that fatal hour. For justice here was fully satisfied in the just punishment of sin. And mercy triumphed and was pleased because hereby salvation for poor sinners was effected."

My doxologies continued to flow, "Oh, Eternal Praises to His Holy Name forever! that His Grace has made me will to accept this salvation and thereby to become an heir to glory. For I shall ever remember some of those **lost Wretches** here have, in their bitter lamentations urged that when salvation has been offered them, they refused it. It was therefore grace alone that helped me to accept it."

And now, before I do put up my pen,
I'll show the profit of my book, and then
Commit both thee, and it unto that hand
That pulls the strong down,
And makes weak ones stand.

It shows too who sets out for life amain,
As if the lasting crown they would attain:
Here also you may see the reason why
They lose their labour, and like fools do die.

John Bunyan

Chapter XIII

Journey of Journeys Ended

While offering my extolment, my Shining Guardian told me hereupon that he must now conduct me to the earth again. And that he would leave me there to wait with faith and patience till my expected happy change should come. "Come then," said he, "and let us leave these realms of woe and horror to the possession of their doleful inhabitants."

On earth again

In a very little space of time I found myself on earth again. I was in that **very place** where I designed to have committed that black sin of being my own murderer, overcome by the temptations of the Devil, who had persuaded me there was no God.

Now what way it was that I came thither, I am not at all able to determine. As soon as I was by the bank that I before had sat on, the Bright Appearance by whom I had been all along conducted, said to me, "Now, Epenetus (Bunyan), you know where you are, and I must stay no longer with you."

My Bright Conductor explained, "I have another ministration to attend. Praise Him that sits upon the Throne Forever, who has **all power** in Heaven, Earth, and Hell, for all the wonders of His love and grace that He has shown you in so short a space." While preparing my response to him, my Guardian Angel disappeared, and I was left alone.

Sense of time lost

Having for some time considered the amazing visions I had seen and the wondrous things that I had heard, I scarce believed I was again on earth. *Neither did I know what time it was I had been absent.*

Humbled

I kneeled down and prayed that I might never lose a lovely sense of all those wondrous things that had been shown me. I then rose up again, blessing and praising God for all His goodness.

Family's unexampled reception

Being returned unto my house, my family was much surprised to see my countenance *strangely changed*. They looked upon me as if they scarce had known me. I asked them what the meaning was of their unusual admiration. They answered that it was the change in my face that caused it. "In what respect," said I, "is it that I am altered so?"

They told me, "Yesterday your looks were so extremely clouded and cast down you seemed the very image of despair. Now your face appears abundantly more beautiful, and carries all the marks of **perfect joy** and satisfaction in it."

"If you had seen," said I, "what I have seen today, you would not wonder at the change you see." Then going into my closet, I took my pen and ink and there wrote down what I had heard and seen, declaring the visions from first to last — **all which I hope may have the same effect on those that read them, as they had on me in writing them.** End

Editing this manuscript has pierced even to the dividing asunder of soul and spirit. My conscience has been awakened. Heaven has become more real, Hell more hostile; life more precious, and the hereafter more revered.

Questions remaining unanswered after initial readings were made plain in later proofings.

May all who read be equally impacted for truly
John Bunyan
". . . being dead yet speaketh," Heb. 11:4.

Mary Stewart Relfe

SALVATION?

If you sincerely desire to know God:

Admit the problem (You are a sinner.) —
Romans 3:23
Realize the penalty for sin —
Romans 6:23
Understand God's provision for you —
Romans 5:8   John 3:16
Accept God's promise of forgiveness, and
Confess your sins,
I John 1:9
Repent (be sorry enough to turn from your
sins)
II Corinthians 5:17
Believe and *Receive* Christ as your Savior
Romans 10:9-10   John 1:12

If you have received Jesus Christ in your heart
as a result of reading this book, we would like to
pray for you and send you helpful Christian mate-
rials. Please fill in and mail.

NAME: _____

ADDRESS: _____

CITY: _____

STATE: _____ **ZIP** _____

OTHER BOOKS
By
Mary Stewart Relfe

☐ When Your Money Fails, 666 $ 6.00
☐ The New Money System $ 7.00
☐ Cure of All Ills — Revival $ 7.00
☐ Should You Take a Little Wine? $ 4.00
☐ Make Known His Deeds $ 3.00
☐ League of Prayer Newsletter   Free

OUTSTANDING VIDEOS
Prayer and Miracles
(Order on next page)

L) Dr. David Yonggi Cho
interviewed by
R) Mary Stewart Relfe
on —

- Dr. Cho's visit in heaven
- Dr. Cho's assistant — 3 days in heaven
- Prayer life at Yoido Full Gospel Church

VIDEOS

☐ **PRAYER & MIRACLES** $ 35.00
   (75 min.)
☐ **LET US PRAY**   (35 min.) $ 20.00
   Dr. Mary Stewart Relfe
   praying/speaking
   (with Dr. Cho)

AUDIO TAPES
By
Mary Stewart Relfe

☐ I Saw Children in Hell $ 5.00
☐ Ravens Cry — People Pray $ 5.00
☐ Please send Book/Tape List
              Postage/Handling $ 2.00
              Total Order $ _____

Name _____

Address _____

City _____

State _____   Zip _____

☐ Ck./MO ☐ Visa/MC Exp. Date _____

Card # _____

Signature _____

Prayer Requests

*" . . . All things whatsoever you shall ask in
prayer believing, you shall receive,"
Mat. 21:22.*

_____

_____

_____

_____

_____

_____

_____

_____

_____

Name _____

Address _____

City _____ **ST** ____ **Zip**_____

Telephone _____

Quotes

Governor —

FOB JAMES, JR.
GOVERNOR

STATE OF ALABAMA
GOVERNOR'S OFFICE
MONTGOMERY

March 11, 1996

*"I am happy for the opportunity to speak on Dr. Relfe's behalf, and to recommend her and her work…" I particularly recognize her fine integrity, her outstanding character, and her dedication to humanitarian causes…which are used to uplift society both here and abroad in the name of our Lord… **Dr. Relfe is a friend from whom I have sought guidance during times that I've had to make hard decisions…"***

Fob James, Jr.

Auditor —

I can truthfully testify that Dr. Relfe is a lady of extremely high ethical standards. In all of my experience as an auditor I have never seen operational efficiencies such as exist at League of Prayer. Administrative costs are the lowest of any nonprofit organization's expenses I have ever seen. The financial records are impeccable. . ."

Steve Richardson, CPA
Tuscaloosa, Alabama
(2-6-96)

Dr. Cho —

"I believe this League of Prayer is born of the Holy Spirit and no man can stop it . . . the future is explosive . . . I believe God will use Dr. Relfe and this League of Prayer to change America and the whole world, for prayer moves the hand that moves the world."

Dr. Yonggi Cho, pastor of world's largest church, Yoido Full Gospel, speaking at a League of Prayer Convention.

Pastor Osteen —

"What a blessing you have been to me and my family, and to Lakewood Church here in Houston, TX . . .

"I'm so glad God has led you to found the League of Prayer which I believe is destined to help change the course of local churches, our nation and other nations of the world . . .

*"It is so evident that you wear the mantle to fulfill the ministry that God has given you. **The power of the Holy Ghost comes like a flame upon you as you walk in obedience to this vision.** The world needs ministries and people like you who have a heart for the world and walk in integrity and honesty . . . "*

Pastor John Osteen,
Lakewood Church, Houston, TX
(6-28-96)

Notes